Just talk with God

Eight ways to change your life

Courtney R. Smith

Just talk with God

Eight ways to change your life

Courtney R. Smith

FIRST EDITION

ISBN-978-0-578-66496-5

For my Mom and Dad

and my Dear friend Eloise

If any of you lacks wisdom, you should ask God, who gives generously to all without finding fault, and it will be given to you."

James 1:5 (NIV)

Foreword

Give ear to my words, O Lord, consider my meditation. Hearken unto the voice of my cry, my King, and my God: for unto thee will I pray.

Psalm 5:1-2 (KJV)

It was a cool October day when I broke down at the office and called my sister and best friend. She answered right away and immediately sensing my pain, she asked "What's wrong?" After pulling myself together, I explained to her how I had reached my breaking point in my then current position. "I hate this job and I can't do it anymore!" Is how I responded as the tears flowed down my face. At that moment, I was prepared to walk completely away from my only source of income at the time. She understood my pain and it pained her to hear me so upset. She reminded me that I have to keep praying and wait on the Lord to move me to my next designation in life. I wasn't too thrilled to hear those words, but I could not deny the truth that soaked through them. I quickly pulled myself together, said a prayer, and walked back into that office with my head held high, and declared I would not allow the enemy to defeat me in the workplace.

When I returned to my desk, I had four hours left until I was able to clock out and go home for the day. I looked at the workload before me and asked God for the strength to complete my tasks and also get me through the day. Eight hours of the same tedious tasks performed at forty hours a week was beginning to take a toll on me. Mentally, physically, and spiritually

I was drained. I was grateful to find this particular position and thanked God constantly for giving me a job. However, I also felt that this was something that tore down my spirit. Every morning, I found myself doing one of the things Christians shouldn't do.That is to complain! I complained, complained, and complained until it was out of style. "Lord I can't do this" "Lord you have to find me something else", "Oh God, I can't do this job!" Those are a few of the complaints that I often allowed to leave my mouth. I grew irritated as I got dressed and prepared to commute on my normal forty minute drive to the office. The traffic alone was enough to make me scream. I would beat myself up for allowing myself to even apply to a position so far from home. At the time, I was seeking employment. I sought better pay, better benefits, and a new position overall. I prayed and asked God to bless me and of course he came through for me and I landed the job. Nineteen months later, I found myself in the wilderness, stuck at job I despised, and filled with stress and anxiety about how I was going to over come this. Furthermore, I knew I had to make a change to define my destiny while in the wilderness.

Now it is time to talk with God! In this book, I will share with you a part of my journey in the wilderness and how I learned to change my life by doing eight simple things. I will keep it short and sweet. I think it is amazing how our words can help shape our life. When we talk with God we are making room for our blessings. I believe that if you follow these eight principles you will have a new perspective on life. However, I can't advise that it will be an easy journey and that healing will immediately come in your life and that miracles will flood your life if you read this book. What I can do is remind you that we serve a God that is bigger than anything or anyone! When we announce ourselves as believers we have a duty to uplift other believers and worship with each other. God has placed these words on my heart to share with others who may have some of my same struggles or those who simply wonder when God will answer their prayers? I'm here to tell you friends, that if you are in the wilderness you are much closer to your blessings and breakthroughs than you could ever imagine! God has great things in store for you but he will also allow your faith to be tested. You may face trials and tribulations in life, but it is light at the end of the tunnel. So hang in there and wait on God no matter the situation.

1

Stop Complaining

Often when we find that things don't go our way or God hasn't answered our prayers. What do we do? We simply complain! Sometimes I'm guilty of complaining when things don't work out as planned. Besides, complaining can only make matters worse. It actually distracts us from hearing Gods voice. Regardless of how we feel. We should not complain about our unanswered requests, jobs, relationships, money, circumstances, or whatever else that upsets us. Instead we should embrace those challenges as difficult as they may be and view them as a challenge to get where we need to be! We should wake up and declare to our situations that they won't have a place in our life. For instance, you may have felt like me at one point and time in your career. As mentioned, you could often hear me say how I hated my job, how I couldn't do it anymore etc. Let's declare to change our perspective, instead we can say. "Lord, this may not be my dream job, but it's a job. It allows me to support my family and pay my bills. So I'm thankful" Or "Lord, I know you will bless me with something far greater. This is only a portion of what you have yet to do in my life". Just the simple arrangement of our words have power. If only we can believe that and declare that on our lives, we will see great things happen. God said that we could ask him for anything and if it is his will he will grant it to us. So instead of complaining, try asking God to fix the things that you complain about.

"If ye shall ask anything in my name, I will do it"

John 14:16 (KJV)

What Good does complaining do?

Complaining does nothing for us, but sets us back. People complain as if it will make things change. It definitely won't make God act faster on our behalf, but it could delay our blessings. How can we expect God to answer our prayers if we always complain? How will complaining fix our problems? Blessed people aren't complainers. God notices how we handle situations and how we keep our faith when things get rough. If we can't be content with the things in our life how can we be satisfied when God decides to bless us?

Note: Complaining can displease the lord.

"And when the people complained, it displeased the Lord: and the Lord heard it, and his anger was kindled, and the fire of the Lord burnt among them, and consumed them that were in the uttermost parts of the camp"

Numbers 11:1 (KJV)

As believers we have to avoid complaining about our circumstances. The last thing that we would ever want to do is displease the lord! Unlike the children of Israel, we have to trust that God will move on our behalf, if we obey him and don't complain. Only if the children of Israel could have saw the light in their situation. They were confined into years of bondage and pure torture and set free only to complain. It sounds crazy. If we look closely at the situation and completely analyze it, we will see that the wilderness was a far greater option for the children of Israel than slavery. Personally, I would rather travel through the wilderness than spend years of my life enslaved! The children of Israel complained so much and refused to wait on the Lord for their blessings. Instead they thought it would be better to return to Egypt, the land were they suffered. Who would ever want to return to a place of bondage? The children of Israel, sure did! They found the strength to complain about being stuck in the wilderness with Moses. If you find yourself in a rough situation, ask God to move on your behalf before you complain.

"And wherefore hath the Lord brought us unto this land, to fall by the sword, that our wives and our children should be a prey? Were it not better for us to return into Egypt? And they said one to another, Let us make a captain, and let us return into Egypt"

Numbers 14:3-4 (KJV)

So take a stand and decide to be faithful to God and find peace in your current situation. Maybe you are currently living somewhere that is undesirable or drive a car that's not so fancy. Say to yourself, "God thankful for providing me shelter. I'm thankful that I do not have to live under a bridge". "Thank you Jesus for providing me with transportation to get me from A to B". When we show God we are thankful for the things we already have. We simply open the door to allow him to bless us with so much more.

From this moment on make a vow to God and let him know you will no longer complain, no matter what the situation looks like. God is good and he is always gracious even when we don't realize it. Remember complaining gets us no where but only slows us down!

Prayer: Father, forgive me for complaining. I vow to not complain and I vow to allow you to work miracles in my life. Help me to control my thoughts before I open my mouth to complain. I promise to trust you and quit complaining. Amen.

Notes

2

Trust and believe that God can perform the impossible

"Trust in the lord with all thine heart; and lean not unto thine own understanding"

Proverbs 3:5 (KJV)

As believers we say that we believe that God can do great works and that he can move any mountain. But honestly how many of us can say that we truly believe that, when we still doubt and don't fully trust God? We worship and we praise the Lord, and at the same time we don't trust him to do the impossible. Instead we listen to the words and logic of this world. It doesn't matter what the medical report said or what our finances say. God can change things in a heartbeat. He is the only one that we can trust to work miracles in our life.

Even as a woman of God, I still find myself filled with doubt. While I pursued my Bachelors degree at the University of Missouri, I felt that I would never graduate, I would never finish my degree, never past my complex courses. There were times were I simply wanted to give up. Why couldn't I just trust God and believe that he would carry me though my obstacles and also give me the strength to handle them? Now that I look back at my life, I can honestly say I would have saved myself a lot of grief as a student if I would have trusted God.

How can we trust God when everything seems to be going wrong in our lives?

Maybe the rent is past due, your child is acting up in school, your spouse left, the job laid you off, your vehicle is on it's last leg, or the bills are piling up and you can't seem to get ahead. Maybe the business you started isn't going well, or maybe it's taking you longer to complete your degree than you anticipated. Whatever the situation is, it's not too big that God can't get you out of it. Allow yourself to trust God in your time of despair, and don't spend time trying to figure out why things aren't working out. Trust me, I tried numerous times to figure out why certain things happened the way they happened in my life, but it didn't do me any good.

Just as the old saying goes. "Nothing worth fighting for will be easy". Some things in life will be a challenge. Please keep that in mind as you travel through your journey. I'm sorry it's not the way the world works. Every time life doesn't go our way we can't throw the towel in and remove ourselves from the fight. As a child, that may have worked, but as we grow physically and spiritually in the Lord we must learn to trust God. *Proverbs 3:5*, is a very crucial verse to us as Christians. I always find comfort reading that verse when I seem to face difficulties. I may not understand the things that are happening, but I can find peace when I put my trust in the Lord.

Please don't be troubled by what isn't working. Put your focus on God and watch him work. I can recall a time, when I was really stressed out over a large medical bill I accumulated from a short stay in the hospital. I began to stress and worry on how big the amount was and how I was never going to be able to pay off this debt. I worried about it appearing on my credit as an unpaid debt and the several pas due notices I received in the mail frightened me. As I read the amount on the paper, I pondered on how it was impossible for me to pay off a large amount of money in short period of time. My thought process was, "This amount is impossible to pay off. There is no way they can expect me to pay that within that timeframe. Lord why didn't my insurance cover this?" On the contrary, my thought process should have been, "Indeed this amount is impossible for me to pay off, but nothing is impossible for my God!"

Nevertheless, a short while later, I received a revised bill in the mail. It was a bill showing that almost one hundred percent of my debt had been paid! I was simply amazed and instantly knew it was God! Who else could do such an amazing thing? I thanked God for his mercy and kindness towards me as I read the remaining balance on my statement of seven dollars and fifty cents! Yes you read it correctly, seven dollars and fifty cents was all I had to pay to settle my debt. I absolutely wasn't going to dispute that! I quickly sent in the remaining balance and settled my debt. Isn't God good? Even with my doubts, God still stepped in and did the impossible! As a reminder of God's mercy, I kept the bill of seven dollars and fifty cents to show that God can do the impossible.

"And we know that all things work together for good to them that love God, to them who are called according to his purpose"

Romans 8:28 (KJV)

As a believer what will you do to make sure you are allowing God to work?
Will you completely trust him? Will you still trust him when things don't go as planned?

Prayer: Lord I put my trust in you. I know that you can move mountains and perform the impossible in my life. Lord please continue to bless me and my family. I love and I trust you to perform miracles in my life.

Notes

3

Stop comparing yourself to others

"Indeed, the very hairs of your head are all numbered. Don't be afraid; you are worth more than many sparrows"

Luke 12:7 (KJV)

You are amazing and worth so much to God! Before we even breathed life, God had already formed us in his image and perfected us to his likings. He even took the time to count the hairs on our head, because he loves us more than we can imagine! If only we could see ourselves, the way God sees us, we will see our true beauty and recognize our worth!

How can we do so?

First, we must stop comparing ourselves to each other. Myself included, I have compared myself to others and sometimes felt unworthy. The society we live in, doesn't really allow us much room to not compare ourselves to others. Every time we turn on the TV, listen to the radio, read an article in the magazine. We are flooded with images and advertisements that remind us how different we are from others. Being different is perfectly fine, in fact it is the way God intended for us to be. He made your skin the color it is for a reason. Your particular shape is unique. Your hair is the way God designed it to be. Your imperfections are perfect in God's eyes. Your features are hand picked from God himself! Keep in mind that God makes no mistakes! You don't need enhancements, plastic surgery or anything else you may feel you are lacking. If God wanted you to look a certain way, he would have made you that way.

Secondly, when comparing ourselves to others we must not focus on money or material possessions. We either love the Lord or we love the things of this world. We can't be lukewarm in that area. Either we are on God's team or we are against him. It is up to you to decide which choice you will make. Pay close attention to the verse below.

"No man can serve two masters: for either he will hate the one, and love the other; or else he will hold to the one, and despise the other. You cannot serve both God and money"

Matthew 6:24 (KJV)

You may struggle with compassion to others if you ever find yourself ever asking these questions below. Often I hear people complain and question God when they compare themselves to others. When things don't go as they planned, they begin to lack faith and make comparisons. It seems as if their faith goes away when they question God. So take a moment and ask yourself how often you make comparisons. It's okay if you do, we are all human and we often become curious. Just try not to make it a habit of questioning God when things seem out of place. Just take a seat and let God work.

Why do bad things happen to good people and not bad people?

Why does it seem that some people are blessed and others are not?

Why can't I have a nice car?

Why can't I have a nice big house?

Why can't I have the perfect job?

Why can't I be beautiful/ handsome like so and so?

Why couldn't I be successful like so and so?

Why can't I have a happy marriage/relationship?

Why does it seem that some people get away with things and I can't catch a break?

It happened for so and so why can't it happen for me?

Comparison can be tough if we allow it to cloud our judgement. I can't provide an explanation to any of these questions. What I can do is remind you that God did not intend for us to live in comparison, nor does he desire for us to feel less significant in comparison to others. One way to help you escape the wilderness is to stop the comparison. We will never be like others no matter how hard we try or how we try to alter our lives. We aren't meant to be the same, even identical twins are born with different fingerprints. God made sure that there is only one you! No matter what the enemy tells you or what your insecurities say, you are special and you are significant to God. You just have to believe that and understand that he only wants what is right for you. Not what your neighbor has, not what your friend has, not what your co-worker has, or what your sibling has, but only what is designed for you!

Prayer: Dear Lord, thank you for creating me to your perfection. You made me unique, special, and beautiful in my own way. I am one of a kind and cannot be duplicated! I am yours and there is no one like me. I will not compare myself to others or strive to be perfect. I am created by the most high and I'm amazing!

Notes

4

Stop Worrying

"Fear thou not; for I am with thee: be not dismayed; for I am thy god: I will strengthen thee; yea, I will help thee; yea, I will uphold thee with the right hand of my righteousness"

Isaiah 41:10

Why do we worry? What does worrying do for us?

We worry because we have been taught that if we don't have certain things then something is wrong in our life. Society has programmed us to think that we have to achieve certain things in life to be successful or satisfied with our lives. If we don't have enough money, the right car, the perfect house then we must be doing something wrong? We must program ourselves to reshape our thinking. Once we reshape our thinking we reshape our destiny.

The first step we must take is to stop worrying. When we trust God and realize he is in full control and worrying is irrelevant. Worrying only adds stress and negativity to soak through. Once the negative thoughts and worry make their way in our minds, it becomes more difficult to get rid of them. However, if we take the approach to leave worry behind then we are reshaping our thought process.

For those who constantly worry, what has worry done for your life? Has it made you stronger? Has it made you more capable? No it hasn't and it never will. Leave worry behind just as Jesus did with the disciples in the storm. I found it to be amazing how they panicked and filled their minds with fear while Jesus sat right there with them! Jesus stayed calm and didn't become afraid because he knew he was in full control. As followers of Christ, we can take that same approach and allow God to rescue us from the storms in life. There is no need to worry while we have God on our side.

"Can any one of you by worrying add a single hour to your life?"

Matthew 6:27 (NIV)

Prayer: Father, forgive me for worrying. I can't add any value to my life by worrying. Regardless of what my circumstances say I am blessed. Worry has no place in my life. I will not worry, instead I will trust you! Amen.

Notes

5

Obey God and his commandments

"Now therefore, if ye will obey my voice indeed, and keep my covenant, then ye shall be a peculiar treasure unto me above all people: for all the earth is mine"

Exodus 19:5 (KJV)

If we are truly followers of God, we will easily obey him and follow his commandments. First, we must allow ourselves to sit back and allow God to take the drivers seat. We can't win if we keep disobeying everything he instructs us to do. God placed it on my heart and mind to create this book. I have other books that I have written which are not Christian books. So why did I decide to write this one? God spoke to me and advised me this is the book that can inspire others who face similar situations. If God can help me then he surely can help you.

In order for God to move on our behalf, he will test us and make sure we are ready and also test us to see if we can follow his commandments. I have been in the wilderness before, and prayed and asked God to deliver me. Of course, he delivered me just as I asked. However, I would find myself back into the wilderness feeling lost and confused. Why? All because I did not follow God's commandments. Often I begged God for ways out of certain situations, received God's help and only to find myself being the same. I'm not talking about changing your wardrobe, upgrading your lifestyle or making drastic changes. Only drastic changes you should allow should be the drastic change in your spiritual self. Change your core and change how you listen and respond to God. When he calls you, just as a Father calls his child, you should listen and obey his will.

"Therefore if any man be in Christ, he is a new creature: old things are passed away, behold, all things are become new"

2 Corinthians 5:17 (KJV)

What happens when we don't obey his commandments?

We all know, not following God's commandments can lead us in the wrong direction in life. When God bails us out of a situation, he desires us to live a new life and be a new creation. Not go back into sin, or live the same way. For example, when we get up in the morning to start our day. We don't pull out dirty clothes and wear them to work or school and expect people to greet us with open arms. Instead, we bathe, iron our clothes, and groom ourselves before stepping out into the world. Just as we start fresh to begin a new day, God expects us to start fresh with him. When God pulls you out of that situation, whatever it may be, it is best that you obey him and keep his commandments. After he has pulled you out of the wilderness and allowed you to be free. It becomes your job to be a new creation and not live the way you have been living. Don't become like the children of Israel, instead accept your blessings when God pulls you from the wilderness. Allow that to be the sign for you to change your life and follow God's commandments. Don't allow the enemy to pull you back into a trap and lead you down the wrong path. We are aware of God's commandments and we should make it our duty to follow them. Try keeping a note to yourself or print them out to make sure you are always following his commandments.

Read Exodus 20 to review God's commandments.

Take a moment and review these study questions to help you as you prepare to obey God and his commandments.

Do I understand God's commandments?

Will I keep God's commandments?

Will I allow the enemy to prevent me from following God's commandments?

How can I be example for my children or my family?

Will I do whatever it takes to follow God?

Prayer: Dear Lord, forgive me for my sins. I love you and I vow to obey your commandments. You know what is best for me and you have my whole life in your hands. From this moment on, I will obey your commandments. Amen.

Notes

6

Always put God first

"But see ye first the kingdom of God, and his righteousness; and all these things shall be added unto you"

Matthew 6:33 (KJV)

Yes putting God first is extremely important as a Christian. If we expect for God to work in our lives and bring us out of our wilderness we have to put him first. Yes first! First over everything in our lives. Remember it is God who blessed us with our family, our cars, our houses, jobs etc. Putting God first should be easy, since he is such a loving and gracious God. If you truly love God and you acknowledge him as your Lord and Savior, it won't be difficult to put him first. When we talk about putting him first, that means first in every area of your life! All we have to do is follow his word, and put him first and he will give us the desires of our hearts. Yes it's that simple! Obey God and put him first and he will bless you far greater than anyone could imagine.

God must be first in every aspect of our lives. Start by putting God first in your finances. Yes your money belongs to God! All that you have, it comes from the Lord. There is nothing on this earth that doesn't belong to God. Don't allow society to disrupt your thinking and cause you to believe that earthly possessions belong to us. Yes in reality, if you buy something legally from the store you are considered the owner. Well that's not completely true.

Everything belongs to God. The stars, the moon, the Sun and everything on Earth is the Lords. Read the verse below carefully.

"The earth is the Lord's, and everything in it, the world, and all who live in it"

Psalms 24:1 (NIV)

As the verse above states, everything in the world belongs to the Lord. We must emphasize the word "everything" and realize that there is nothing on this earth that doesn't belong to him. Nothing or no one, no thing, no creature, no land, anything! You and I belong to the Lord and we always will.

When we put him first in our finances we show God that he can trust us and that when we do get riches we won't run off and forget about God. Obviously, God doesn't need our money nor does he care about how much money we have. He wants to know that we are faithful to him and that we can trust to put him first financially.

If you are still struggling to give to God the very first tenth of your wages, then you don't trust him completely. He only asks for ten percent! Just ten percent! You can give as much as you like, but God simply asks us to give our ten percent from the first fruits of our labor. I'm not talking about paying our light bill, rent, car notes, daycare, then giving God whatever is left over. It's just not fair to God. How would you feel if your loved one went to a fancy restaurant, ate a delicious meal and then brought you home the scraps to eat. Imagine that they picked over all the food and ate everything good from the dinner and then left you with the leftovers. How would you feel? I assume not good. Well that is similar to how we can make God feel in our giving. Wouldn't you like to give God the best? Wouldn't you want to give him the steak and potatoes and not the scraps? Of course, because he desires it and more!

Don't stress yourself out over how you will pay your bills or take care of expenses if you give to the Lord. The Lord is a provider and he is always on time. I have yet to struggle with taking care of things when I give God my first fruits. Yes it's not always comfortable to give, but it is required from us if we are true believers of Christ. Some of us struggle financially not because we are lazy or we don't know how to budget, but because we don't trust God with our tithes and therefore he allows us to see the struggle when we don't give to him. That money you received from your paycheck is the Lords. He is the one who gives us breath in our body and strength to make it to work everyday. If you try to rob God by withholding your tithes, God can still find a way to make sure he gets his offering.

"And that we should bring the firstfruits of our dough, and our offerings, and the fruit of all manner of trees, of wine and of oil, unto the priests, to the chambers of the house of our God; and the tithes of our ground unto the Levites, that the same Levites might have the tithes in all the cities of our tillage."

Nehemiah 10:37 (KJV)

I can recall a time, that I felt uneasy and nervous paying my tenth. I said things like, well if I give my tenth, I won't have enough to pay this or that". I wanted to give, but I was afraid. Afraid I would go without and not be able to take care of things. So I made the mistake of not giving my tenth and decided I would use that money to pay a bill instead. Nevertheless, it was a big mistake on my behalf. What was I thinking, trying to withhold from God? As I discovered, the money that I was supposed to give for tithing, I received an unexpected expense for the same amount. How strange I thought to myself. The moment I thought I was getting away from tithing, is the moment it backfired on me. I thought I could skip my tithing, and take care of my expenses, then give God what is left over. No, it just doesn't work that way. I ended up in a bind, because I still had to take care of other things, and now I had a extra expense! I said to myself, "Wow I should have just gave my tithe". My unexpected expense was the exact amount of my tenth. How easy it would have been to just pay God what belongs to him and just keep going. However, I made it more difficult on myself the moment I decided to not give. I felt guilty and silly about it. From that moment on, I saw that as a lesson from God. I made sure that I gave to God first, then pay my bills and expenses last. Please don't rob God by holding out. You may think you can get away and keep extra money if you don't pay your tithes but you can't. God will put holes in your finances and get what is owed to him. Besides, wouldn't you rather give to the Lord, then have unexpected expenses hurting your pockets?

We all have expenses and bills, but when we trust in God we allow him to bless our finances and make a way for us. God will always provide a way for you, as long as you are faithful to him and give your tithe and offering. Just as God paid for my medical expenses, he can work miracles in your life as well.

Prayer: Lord forgive me for all the times I did not put you first in my life. I trust you and believe that you know what is best for me. I will put you first in every aspect of my life. Everything I have comes from you. Lord I am thankful and grateful to have you in my life. Amen.

7

Learn to let go

Letting go can be one of the most difficult things we have to face in life. No matter what stage we are in life. Letting go is often a drastic change we may have to endure. As we grow in faith, we must understand that letting go is a critical part of the process that will help us get to where we need to be. Just those words alone can make us reflect and analyze our lives as we acknowledge whatever it is that we must let go.

Letting go is usually never easy because it causes us to remove ourselves from our comfort zones and our familiar territory. From my personal experience, I found that letting go is very significant and it has opened me up to brand new experiences and opportunities.

If we take a moment to understand the process of letting go we can break it down from a worldly perspective. For instance, if you are currently working but you are seeking new opportunities. Let's say, one day a new opportunity comes your way and you have to make a decision. You will need to leave your current position where you know what to expect and it is everything you're familiar with. On the contrary, the new opportunity is everything you have been praying for or maybe it is a resolution to your current financial state. Maybe you need better hours, a closer location, or a new career path. Whatever the reason is you will have to leave one of those opportunities behind. In theory, what will you find yourself doing? The answer is simple, usually you will let go of your current job to move on to a much greater opportunity. You can't choose both realistically, so you will allow for one to escape while you hold on to the other. This is the first step in the process of letting go.

The same way we let go of things in our life is the same way we need to learn to let go in our spiritual life. When God is calling us to grow, he wants us to change and see things from a bigger perspective. Whatever it is in your life that you need to let go, you will have to make that decision. No one can decide for you. For some it may be a job you're comfortable at, or maybe it is a habit you can't seem to let go. What if it is a friend who you must depart from? Maybe you no longer see eye to eye or maybe that person's interests and beliefs are no longer aligned with yours. Maybe it is an addiction that you must remove from your life. Maybe it is drugs and or alcohol. It can even be your way of thinking. No matter what the case is, God has the ability to help you let it go if you are willing.

If you take a moment to analyze and reflect God will easily point out the things that you must let go. Just take a quiet moment with God and allow him to speak to you through your heart. When those things that are holding you back come to mind, you will have a clear understanding on what you need to let go of. Once you realize what it is, you can begin the process of change and expand into the person God has called you to be.

Prayer: Dear father, thank you for your blessings and everything you do. I open my heart to you and I ask that you reveal whatever it is to me that you desire for me to let go. If it is a person, Lord grant me the strength to let that person go . I pray that you grant me the strength to allow everything that is hindering me or unpleasant to you to leave my life. No longer will I be a slave to what is holding me back. Amen.

8

Speak life into your dry bones

"I will make breath enter you, and you will come to life. I will attach tendons to you and make flesh come upon you and cover you with skin; I will put breath in you, and you will come to life. Then you will know that I am the Lord"

Ezekiel 37:5 (NIV)

Over the years I have come across many stories involving people who struggle, it could be financially, suffering from an illness, depression, anxiety, or addictions. In some of those stories there are happy endings, recovery stories, and unfortunately sometimes unhappy endings. Whatever the struggle may be, we will not conquer it with dry bones.

As I recall one evening, as I sat at my computer to put in yet another job application. Hoping that I would be blessed with a new opportunity so that I could leave my stressful job. After months of tiresome applications, job assessments, and interviews. I found myself back at square one and restarting my job search. I tried fixing up my resume, making sure it didn't contain any grammatical errors or typos. Nevertheless, I was tired and overwhelmed with my struggle. As I browsed on the computer, I decided to listen to an online sermon. I heard the words, "If you want your life to change. You must speak life into your dry bones and command them to change". From that moment on, I realized that praying and asking God to help me find a new position that I would enjoy wasn't enough. Nothing is wrong with praying and waiting on God. However, we must speak life into our dry bones and declare a change. Instead of praying to God to heal depression, anxiety, financial burdens and addictions. Command and declare for them to move. If you're feeling anxious and nervous, tell your anxiety that you are a child of God and anxiety has no place in your life. Tell depression to move from your spirit, because God has a plan for your life and it doesn't include depression. Tackle that addiction and demand it to stand down. Speak life over that addiction and allow God to take over. Tell your finances that you are a child of the most high, and that you will be financially stable and not allow your finances to overwhelm you. Heal those dry bones and open your mouth and allow the praises to drown out all negativity and all struggle. No more will any struggle consume you, you will demand and declare that anything dry in your life has no place for you.

Furthermore, I decided to take the advice from the sermon and immediately began praising God and declaring for my dry bones to have life. I prayed that I would no longer be stressed by that job, I would have a new position and I would no longer have to worry about that job. With just a few simple words, I changed the direction of my life. A day or two later I received a phone call for an interview for a job I applied for. I couldn't believe how fast my situation had changed. I scheduled my interview and a week later I landed the job. I knew anything was possible with God, but I never spoke life into my bones to allow my life to change. This isn't just about finding a new job. I'm speaking about changing your life and changing the things in your life. For me one of those things was finding a new job at that time, for you it may be an illness you are suffering with or an addiction. I'm here to tell you that if you don't speak life into your dry bones nothing will happen and you may continue to struggle.

Take charge and tell your illness that you will recover in the name of Jesus. Sickness has no place in your life and you declare for it to leave. Tell that addiction that you are no longer tied down by it and you are set free by the Lord. No weapon or struggle formed against you shall prosper. Your dry bones will be set free, you will prosper and be set free.

I took charge and declared that I would not be stressed and that my new job was just moments away. I kept praying and I kept my faith but the key was to make sure my bones had life. You may ask yourself, how can doing so change my life? Because our words have power just as the bible says, the power of life and death is in the tongue. Be careful of the words that you allow to escape your mouth. Words have power and you have the power to define your destiny by your words!

 Remember that you will stay the same if you are unwilling to change. Praying and hoping won't open you up to God's glory and blessings. You have to work with God and speak life over those dry places in your life if you desire change. Soon enough you will see your breakthrough and the many plans God has for your life! Now go and face the world with a new perspective on life. You're wonderful, smart, and you are the child of the most high! Nothing anyone says about you will matter, it is only what God says about you that matters. Remember he sees the good in you and he is waiting on you to change your life so he can bless you. God will never leave your side. His grace will always surround you if you believe and put him first in your life. No matter where you are in life, you can still change and be who God has called you to be. I recommend trying these eight principles of this book, so you can see how wonderful God is.

I pray that this book has inspired you to keep fighting through obstacles in life and maintain or begin a relationship with Christ. I pray that doors open up for you and that you receive everything that God has planned for you. Declare and define your destiny as you talk with God! Stay blessed!

Now that you have the eight keys to define your faith and build your destiny, it's time to apply those concepts to your life! Take a moment to review these discussions questions and reflect on them deeply. Study with a group or individually.

Discussion Questions

How would you rate your faith on a scale from 1 to 10?

What motivates you to keep trusting in God?

How has God shaped your life?

Do you have a plan to increase your faith in the Lord during hard times?

How committed are you to your tithing?

How often do you complain about your life?

How do you plan to speak life into the dry areas of your life?

Are you prepared to let everything go that is hindering you? Even the things you enjoy the most?

Do you become upset with God when things aren't going as planned?

Do you feel like God ignores you and favors others?

Notes

www.ingramcontent.com/pod-product-compliance
Lightning Source LLC
LaVergne TN
LVHW041210080426
835508LV00008B/884